Reader's Digest READING SKILL BUILDER

SILVER EDITION EDITORS

Miriam Weiss Meyer and Peter Travers, Project Editors

Barbara Aritonopulos and Jacqueline Kinghorn, Editors

SILVER EDITION CONSULTANTS

Fred Chavez, Director of Programs
Los Angeles City Reading Support Services Center
Los Angeles, California

Marguerite E. Fuller, Assistant Supervisor of Language Arts
Norwalk Public Schools
Norwalk, Connecticut

Sister Maria Loyola, I.H.M., Chairperson, Reading Curriculum Committee
Archdiocese of Philadelphia
Philadelphia, Pennsylvania

Dr. John. F. Savage, Coordinator, Reading Specialist Program
Boston College, School of Education
Chestnut Hill, Massachusetts

Richard B. Solymos, Reading Resource Teacher
School Board of Broward County
Fort Lauderdale, Florida

READER'S DIGEST EDUCATIONAL DIVISION
© 1977 by Reader's Digest Services, Inc., Pleasantville, N.Y. 10570. All rights reserved, including
the right to reproduce this book or parts thereof in any form.
Printed in the United States of America.
Reader's Digest ® Trademark Reg. U.S. Pat. Off. Marca Registrada ISBN 0-88300-410-0

■ ■ Part 4

Silver Edition

P9-BJO-841

STORIES

🎧 Stories for which Audio Lessons are available.
RDX number indicates RDX card for that story.

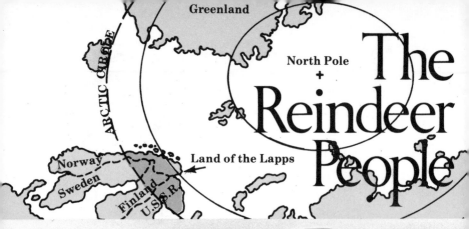

Greenland

North Pole
+

ARCTIC CIRCLE

Land of the Lapps

Norway

Sweden

Finland

U.S.S.R.

The Reindeer People

Key Words

reindeer   Arctic
northern   herd, herding
Lapps   ski, skis

by Lawrence Elliott

Their lives depend on reindeer. They use these animals for both food and clothes. Reindeer are everything to them! Who are these people? They live in the icy northern parts of Europe. They are called Lapps.

The Lapps take care of reindeer. In the summer, the reindeer swim to Arctic islands. In the fall, the reindeer swim back to the mainland. The Lapps must travel through freezing winds and snow while they take care of the reindeer. In summer, the sun never sets for two months. In the winter, it stays dark for two whole months.

The Lapps can do some things better than most people. They see and hear so well that they can tell from far away which deer in a herd are theirs.

Another special thing about the Lapps is that they never get lost in their travels. They can find a place again, even if they haven't been back to it in years! It's as if they carry a map in their minds.

When they are herding reindeer, Lapps sleep in large tents. Three families may share the same tent.

The whole family, even the dogs,

helps with the herding. By ten years of age, a Lapp child can ski over to a reindeer and catch it with a rope.

Every piece of clothing the Lapps wear has a special use. Their clothes are colored so that the Lapps can be seen in the fierce Arctic snowstorms. Their long, pointed hats are used like pockets to carry things. When stuffed with feathers, the hat becomes a pillow. The curled tips of their deerskin boots help to keep their skis in place.

When a family is not traveling, it is getting ready for the next move. The Lapps sew clothes, boots and tents from reindeer skins. Even their thread is made from parts of the reindeer. A Lapp might sew as many as 80 pairs of boots in one year. It is easy to wear out ten pairs of deerskin boots in one winter!

The Lapps eat reindeer meat. They dry some of the meat so they will have food on their next trip. Meat that is dried does not spoil. They even make powdered milk to take with them. Of course, it's reindeer milk. A Lapp family needs to have 200 reindeer just to be sure it will have food and clothing for one year.

Each Lapp family puts a special mark on their reindeer's ears. This mark tells who owns the deer.

Spring is a favorite time of year for the Lapps. It is then that they return home to their villages. There they visit friends and enjoy themselves. Reindeer racing is a popular sport at this time. But this joyful season at home does not last long. Soon the Lapps must head north again to the icy Arctic snow to follow the reindeer.

9

LASSO LAPP WORDS   *vocabulary*

Write the numeral of each word beside its meaning.

1. Arctic
2. herd
3. ski
4. tent

_*1*_ the far north
_*4*_ a group of animals
_*3*_ a piece of wood worn on the foot and used to travel over snow
_*1*_ a building made of cloth or animal skins which can be moved from place to place

104 · Best Score 4 · My Score _____

LAPPLAND   *story elements*

Check (✔) the three things the author told you about the place in which the Lapps live.

10

_✓_ a. freezing winds
_✓_ b. long, pointed hats
_✓_ c. darkness for two months
____ d. reindeer milk
_✓_ e. snowstorms

⟜ 74 • Best Score 3 • My Score _____

LAPP LIFE *fact/opinion*

Write 1 if the sentence is a fact. Write 2 if the sentence tells you the writer's opinion.

_1_ The Lapps sew clothes, boots and tents from reindeer skins.
_2_ It is easy to wear out ten pairs of deerskin boots in one winter!
_1_ In the fall, the reindeer go back to the mainland.

⟜ 44 • Best Score 3 • My Score _____
All Best Scores 10 • All My Scores _____

WHAT DO YOU KNOW? *points of view*

What things does a Lapp know that you don't? What things do you know that a Lapp might not?

I wonder if lapps are someone like indians.

11

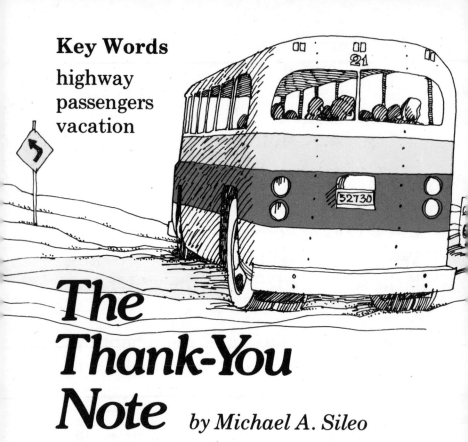

Key Words

highway
passengers
vacation

The Thank-You Note *by Michael A. Sileo*

The big bus hummed along the
highway. The sky was gray, and cold bit
the air. But the 41 passengers were
thinking of <u>sun!</u> Just awhile before,
they had left the city of Boston. Now
they were headed south for a two-week
vacation in sunny Florida.

12

Suddenly the driver felt a heavy, rolling thump under the bus. He stopped the bus at the side of the road.

"What's the matter?" a passenger in back asked.

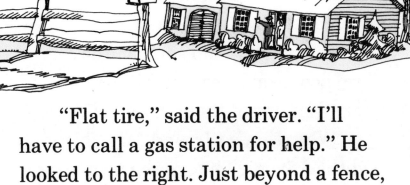

"Flat tire," said the driver. "I'll have to call a gas station for help." He looked to the right. Just beyond a fence, he saw a house. "I'm going over there. Maybe they'll let me use their telephone."

The passengers waited. They worried as the bus grew colder. Soon they saw their driver walking back toward them.

"It's OK," he said as he got aboard. "Someone from the gas station will be here soon."

"Brrrr! I sure hope so!" said one woman. "It's so cold in here, I can see my breath!"

"Hey, look!" said someone else. "Two people are headed this way. Looks as if one of them has a coffee pot!"

"Why, that's Mr. and Mrs. Sileo!" said the driver. "They're the people who let me use their telephone!"

Soon a man and a woman were leaning over the fence. "We thought you might be cold and hungry," called Mrs. Sileo. "So I made a big pot of coffee."

The surprised passengers looked at one another. Then they climbed quickly out of the bus. Mrs. Sileo handed out paper cups and began to pour.

14

"I brought some fresh doughnuts," said Mr. Sileo. "Who would like one?" Eager hands reached out.

By the time the tire was fixed, the passengers were feeling warm and happy again. They climbed aboard their vacation bus. As they pulled back onto the highway, they waved good-bye. Mr. and Mrs. Sileo stood by the fence and waved back.

15

One day two weeks later, Mr. Sileo was looking out the kitchen window. He saw a bus stop on the edge of the highway.

"Looks like another bus with a flat tire," he called to Mrs. Sileo.

She came to the window. "No, the bus is coming up our driveway," she said. "The driver must be lost."

By the time Mr. and Mrs. Sileo got to their front door, a crowd of people were there. All of them were smiling.

"You remember us, don't you?" asked the driver. He handed Mrs. Sileo a big bag. She looked inside. "Oranges!" she said. "But why—?"

"We want to thank you for the coffee and doughnuts," said one passenger.

"But we want to say it in a special way," said another. "Your kindness really got our vacation off to a beautiful start."

"A thank-you note just didn't seem to be enough," said a woman. "So we decided to bring you these oranges from sunny Florida on our way home."

Mr. Sileo took out an orange. He peeled it and handed part of it to his wife.

She bit into the orange. "Mmmmm!" she said. "That's the best thank-you note I ever ate!"

17

RETURN TRIP *skimming*

Circle the word used to tell about each thing. Look in the story for the answers.

1. __a__ sky
   (a.) gray   b. blue

2. __a__ Florida
   (a.) sunny   b. hot

3. __b__ thump
   a. loud   (b.) rolling

4. __a__ doughnuts
   (a.) warm   b. fresh

SAYING THANK YOU *supporting details*

Check (✓) the three things that show the passengers were thankful to the Sileos.

The passengers . . .

____✓ 1. sent a thank-you note.
____✓ 2. stopped especially to see the Sileos.
____✓ 3. ate the doughnuts and coffee.
____✓ 4. smiled at the Sileos.

_____ 5. brought oranges to the Sileos.

WORDS WITH FEELING *sentence meaning*

Circle the letter of the meaning of each sentence.

1. The bus hummed along the highway.
   - a. The bus' engine and tires made a humming noise.
   - b. The bus passengers sang.

2. Suddenly the driver felt a heavy, rolling thump under the bus.
   - a. The bus ran over something.
   - b. The bus had a flat tire.

3. "It's so cold, I can see my breath!"
   - a. The speaker can see very well.
   - b. It's cold in the bus.

HOW DID YOU SAY IT? *comparison/contrast*

Think about a time someone gave you something or did something special for you. How did you say thank you?

I would never forget this day and thank you very much! ☺

19

Key Words

Stromboli
volcanic, volcano
eruption
lava
crater

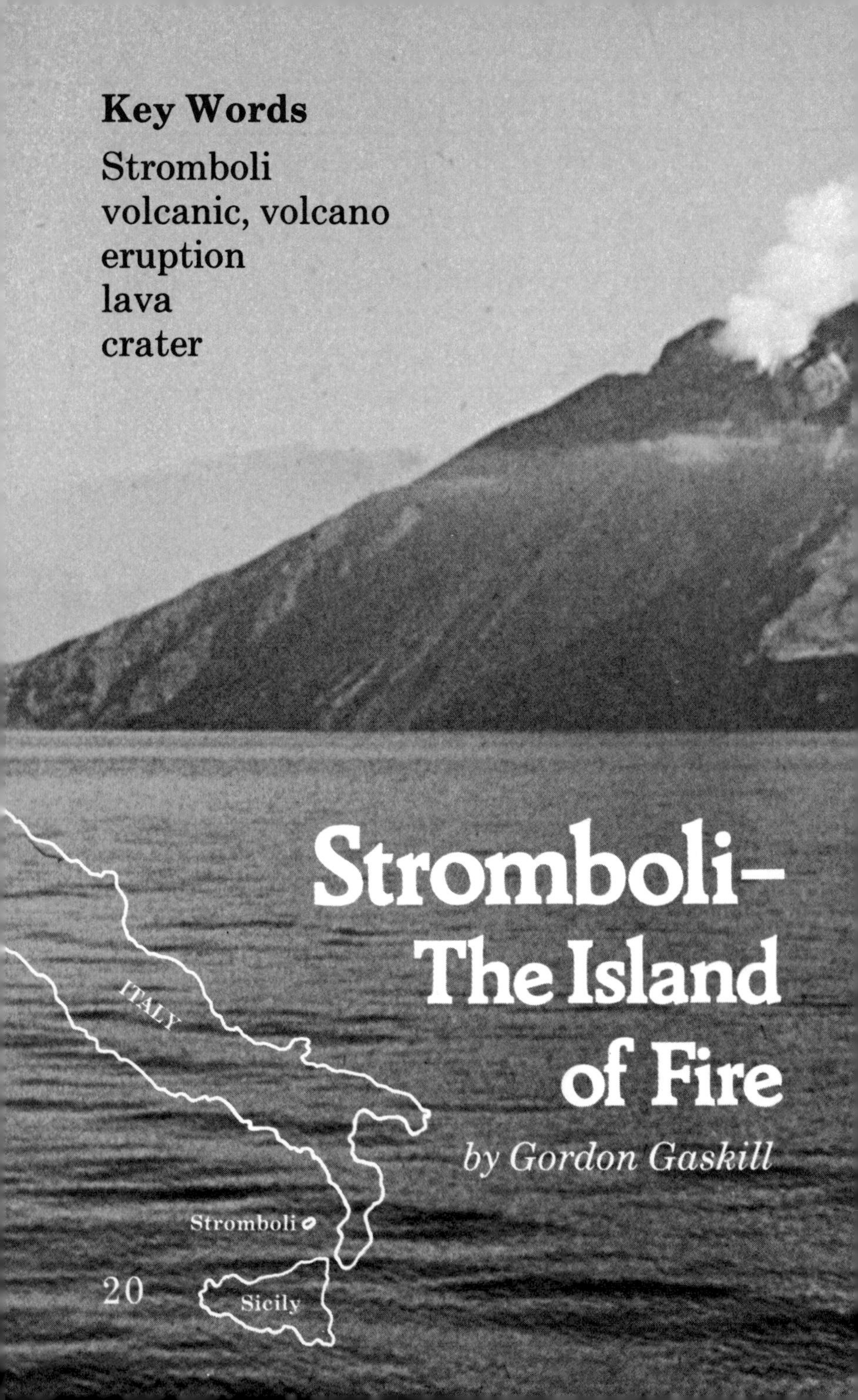

Stromboli– The Island of Fire

by Gordon Gaskill

ITALY

Stromboli

Sicily

I looked out from my boat. Ahead of me was the famous volcanic island I had come so far to see—Stromboli (STRAHM-buh-lee).

I watched the smoke twirl up from the top of the volcano. Stromboli seemed more beautiful than scary. It was like a sleepy, gray-black cat rising from the bright blue sea.

Suddenly the cat moved. Bits of hot, black volcanic rock slid down the side of the volcano. When the rocks hit the water, clouds of steam rose up. The steam made a hissing sound. It was as if the cat-volcano were hissing.

All that noise didn't stop me from landing at one of Stromboli's villages. I found a guide to show me the way to the top of the volcano. The guide's name was Vincenzo (vin-CHEN-zoh).

It took us three hours to walk to the top. There was plenty of time for us to talk about Stromboli.

"Vincenzo, I keep looking up at the smoke. I'm afraid there might be an eruption at any time. We'd never be

A volcano may steam like a kettle . .

able to get away from the steam and smoke and hot *lava* (liquid rock)."

Vincenzo calmed my fears. "Don't worry. It's <u>good</u> that the volcano gets rid of its lava and smoke. Some volcanos keep their lava inside. One day, it gets <u>too</u> hot inside the volcano. All at once, lava and smoke pour out. Rocks come down like rain. The smoke and ash choke people and cover everything."

I asked, "You mean, Stromboli is like a paper bag filled with air? If too much air builds up inside, the bag suddenly bursts."

"Yes. So we like Stromboli to be active," Vincenzo said.

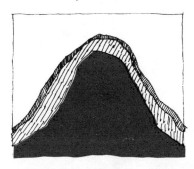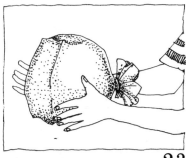

23

. . or pop like a paper bag filled with air.

At last we reached the top. The top of a volcano like Stromboli is not flat or like a hill. It is a *crater* (hole). From the crater come the lava, smoke and steam.

Vincenzo explained about Stromboli. "Stromboli really has <u>two</u> craters. We're standing at the edge of the old crater. Don't worry. We're safe here. This crater is dead. Down there is the new, active crater."

I sat down and watched the "fireworks." Something is always going on. Inside the new crater, four to six "mouths" were working. They spat out lava and steam. Large, red-hot rocks flew through the air. Sometimes big globs of lava or thousands of small stones shot out. All this material usually falls safely back into the crater. Or it slides down to the sea, at the same spot I had seen from my boat.

I stayed up there with Vincenzo for the rest of the day. When we reached the village again, it was dark.

I turned to look back at the volcano. All I could see was a red glow. It seemed warm and friendly to Vincenzo. But I was glad I didn't live on the island of Stromboli. To me, that red glow was a red light warning of danger.

VOLCANIC WORDS *vocabulary*

Write the numeral of each word next to its description.

1. lava   2. crater   3. eruption

_3_ a. hot liquid rock from a volcano

_2_ b. a large hole at the top of a volcano

_1_ c. a burst of steam, hot rock and ash

STROMBOLI *supporting details*

Write the letter of the missing word or words in the blank in each sentence.

Stromboli is _C_.
  a. an island   b. a volcano
  c. both an island and a volcano

To reach the top of Stromboli, you _C_ for three hours.
  a. drive   b. fly   c. walk

Stromboli is like a _b_ filled with air.
  a. balloon   b. paper bag   c. tire

Stromboli has _C_.

a. one dead and one active crater
b. two dead craters
c. two active craters

91 • Best Score 4 • My Score _____

WHO'S SPEAKING?   *signals/antecedents*

Write the numeral of the person or people next to the thing they might have said.

1. the people of Stromboli
2. the author
3. the author and Vincenzo
4. Vincenzo

Who . . . Might Say This?

__1__ a. "*We* don't mind living here."

__2__ b. "Stromboli is too scary for *me*."

__4__ c. "Stromboli doesn't frighten *me*. It's like an old friend."

66 • Best Score 3 • My Score _____

All Best Scores 10 • All My Scores _____

LIVING ON STROMBOLI   *points of view*

If you had been born on Stromboli, would you be afraid to live there? Why?

If I lived in the Stromboli
I kind of be afriad because
I could get killed.

27

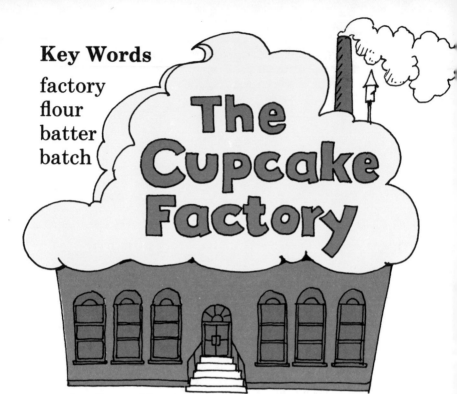

Key Words

factory
flour
batter
batch

The Cupcake Factory

by Lou Kotler Levine

Pretend you work in a cupcake factory! Shut your eyes. Cupcakes sit all over the room. Imagine the great smell!

Workers in a cupcake factory make cakes almost the same way you would make them in your home. The workers mix eggs, sugar, butter and flour. Then they bake the cakes in an oven. But the workers make thousands of cupcakes a day, not just a few. So they need machines to help them.

Machines do most of the big jobs, but workers must watch the machines. They must check to see that the jobs are done right.

There is a machine just for cracking eggs. This machine must crack the eggs gently so that the shells don't fall into the cupcakes. One by one, the

29

eggs roll through the machine. Each egg is cracked, the shells are thrown out and the insides of the eggs are put into the cupcakes.

Then the eggs plop into a huge mixer. A machine shoves a big block of butter into the mixer. Next, big tubs of flour and sugar are dropped in. The mixer whirls and twirls. It turns the butter, eggs, sugar and flour into a smooth batter.

Meanwhile small pans are lined up on a long belt. The belt moves. The batter is dropped into each pan. The

machine knows just how much batter will fit in each pan.

The pans are then sent into a big oven. Soft, warm cupcakes come out in 45 minutes. The cupcakes are left to cool. Next, machines put frosting on each cupcake. The cupcakes are now topped with different colors—pink, white and brown!

Machines can do a lot of important jobs. But there is one job that no machine can do. Only a person can taste a cupcake and say, "Mmmmm, yes, this batch is perfect."

MAKING CUPCAKES *sequence*

Put the sentences in order to show how cupcakes are made.

__4__ Someone tastes the cupcakes.

__3__ The pans go into the oven.

__1__ Butter, eggs, flour and sugar are mixed together.

__2__ Batter is dropped into each pan.

🔑 105 • *Best Score 4* • *My Score* _____

THE GIANT KITCHEN *author's purpose*

Check (✔) two things the author told you about the cupcake factory.

__✓__ 1. The cupcake factory is a big place.

__✓__ 2. The factory needs people to be sure the machines work right.

_____ 3. Cupcakes taste better when they are made in a factory.

🔑 7 • *Best Score 2* • *My Score* _____

32

WHAT AM I? *inferences*

Read each riddle. Put the letter of the answer in the blank. Pick from these machines.

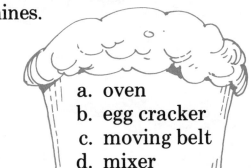

a. oven
b. egg cracker
c. moving belt
d. mixer

_b_ 1. "I am always breaking things."
_a_ 2. "The pans sit on me while they get filled with batter."
_d_ 3. "I turn the butter into batter."
_a_ 4. "Cupcakes couldn't be made if I didn't get hot."

103 · *Best Score 4* · *My Score* _____
All Best Scores 10 · *All My Scores* _____

A DREAM COMES TRUE *prediction*

Would you like to be the worker who tastes cupcakes? Do you think cupcakes would stop being special if you ate them all day? Why or why not? I think they will stop it because the special one are all out and if you made it agian it will be gone

33

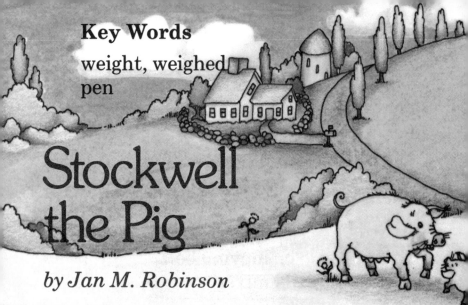

Key Words

weight, weighed
pen

Stockwell the Pig

by Jan M. Robinson

I remember the day Stockwell the pig first came into our lives. It was a cold, rainy afternoon. My family and I were driving past a farmhouse.

"Mom, stop the car!" yelled my kids.

A mother pig and eight baby pigs were crossing the road. After they had passed, my husband said, "Look. There's something lying in that puddle."

We got out of the car. It was a baby pig. He hadn't been strong enough to keep up with his mother. He was alive, but he was too weak to move.

We went up to the farmhouse and showed the farmer the poor little pig. The farmer didn't want the pig. When pigs grow up, they are sold to people who make meat. The farmer didn't think our tiny pig would ever be worth much money. So he gave the pig to us.

We named our pig Stockwell. At first we didn't think he would live. He was weak and thin. He got very sick and almost died.

But we took good care of him. He got well and began to put on weight. Only one bad thing happened to him. One day his funny little curly tail fell off.

Stockwell was an unusual pig. He loved to listen to me playing the piano. He liked me to give him baths in the sink and to rub him with baby oil afterward. He enjoyed car rides.

And he loved the Christmas tree. He thought it was beautiful. He didn't want to leave it. So he slept under the tree every night.

Stockwell ate and ate. He got fatter and fatter. Our "baby" pig soon weighed 300 pounds (136 kilograms). Every time he turned quickly, he knocked a piece of furniture into the wall. We couldn't keep our tail-less, ever-hungry pet in the house any longer. He was too big.

We built a pen for him in the field behind the house. We let him run free a lot, though. He played games with the children. On warm days, he liked to be sprayed with water from the garden hose. He was smart and gentle.

Stockwell was very good at finding bottles. The first one he dug up was worth a lot of money. He put it very carefully next to his food dish. He dug up over 200 bottles that summer and placed each one by the side of his dish.

Stockwell was four years old when we decided to move to another farm that had a lot more land. Of course, Stockwell was to come with us.

Stockwell was much too big to ride in the car. So we decided to take him to the new farm in a truck. We thought he would love a truck ride as much as he did a car ride. We thought he would follow one of us right into the truck.

We were wrong. He wouldn't take one step. He was afraid of the truck.

He lay on the ground. He didn't want to look at that awful truck. He put his front legs over his eyes. He dug his nose into the dirt.

Stockwell wouldn't budge. We had to get two strong workers with ropes to pull him into the truck.

38

When he was safe inside, Stockwell stood as still as a statue. I climbed into the back of the truck to ride with him. As I stood next to him, big tears rolled out of his eyes and down his cheeks.

Today Stockwell is five years old. He is healthy and happy at our new farm. He is also smart and gentle. He likes children and animals. He will even share his food with a cat or chicken.

He has a nice, big pen at the top of a hill. Sometimes he looks down the long, grassy hill. He seems to be thinking about lovely piano music, Christmas trees—and food.

POOR STOCKWELL   *cause/effect*

Each problem below has an answer.
Write the numeral of each problem in
the blank next to its answer.

Problems

1. Stockwell got too fat to live in
   the house.
2. Stockwell got sick.
3. The farmer didn't want Stockwell.

Answers

___3___ The author and her family made
Stockwell a part of the family.

___2___ The family took very good care
of him to make him healthy.

___1___ The family built a pen for
Stockwell in the field.

⌒54 • *Best Score 3 • My Score* _____

FUNNY STOCKWELL   *characterization*

Draw Stockwell's missing tail (℮) next
to the five things that tell you he was
different from most pigs.

Stockwell . . .

___℮___ 1. liked being rubbed with baby oil.

40

_____ 2. liked to eat.

_____ 3. liked piano music.

_____ 4. dug up old bottles.

_____ 5. liked to play games.

_____ 6. could be made into bacon.

_____ 7. would share his food with other animals.

171 • *Best Score 5 • My Score* _____

STOCKWELL'S FAMILY *inferences*

What two things did you learn about the author and her family? Check (✔) them.

The family . . .

___✔___ a. lived in farm country.

_____ b. raised milk cows.

_____ c. had lots of money.

___✔___ d. loved animals.

19 • *Best Score 2 • My Score* _____

All Best Scores 10 • All My Scores _____

OTHER PETS *comparison/contrast*

Do you or someone you know have an unusual pet? What kind of animal is it? Why is it unusual? My friend Melissa has a sheep and it eats like a pig.

41

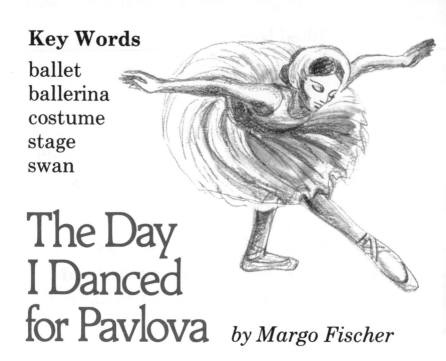

The Day I Danced for Pavlova *by Margo Fischer*

I was in ballet school. One day our dance teacher said to the class, "The great ballerina Anna Pavlova (pahv-LOH-vah) will soon be in a ballet in our city. Three of my best students will dance for her when the ballet is over."

Then our teacher told us the names of the three students she had chosen. Kristina Berg, Lita Chong and me, Margo Fischer. How lucky I was!

But when the special day came, I had a very bad cold. My parents said, "Margo, the ballerina costume is too short and thin to keep you warm. If you go, you'll have to put on long underwear under a dress."

The heavy, long underwear came from under my dress and drooped down onto my shoes. But I wore those ugly clothes to be able to go to the ballet.

That evening my teacher, Kristina, Lita and I went to watch Anna Pavlova dance. Pavlova glided across the stage like a swan on a lake. How happy I felt.

Then it was over. It was time to meet Anna Pavlova. I rolled up the legs of my long underwear. Now they would be hidden under my dress.

Pavlova told our teacher, "I'm very sad today. One of my dear little dogs is dead. But now is no time for feeling sorry for myself. I want to see your students dance."

My teacher had to explain, "Only two of my students can dance. Poor Margo here has a bad cold."

I wanted so much to dance for Pavlova. I pleaded, "Please let me dance."

"Why not let her?" Pavlova asked.

I was filled with joy. I put on the ballet slippers and ran up on stage.

I began. First I ran forward on my toes. Then I spun around as I made a circle around the stage.

I thought I was doing well. But as I circled the stage, I heard people laughing. By the time I was finished, everyone was laughing—even Pavlova.

I looked down and saw what had happened. The legs of my long underwear had fallen down. I had been dancing the whole time in this silly costume.

I jumped down from the stage. I ran to one of the seats in the back of the room and started to cry.

Then I felt a hand under my chin. I looked up into Anna Pavlova's face.

"Don't cry, Margo. You have given me a good laugh. I needed something to cheer me up today. I want to thank you for that. Now listen to me. You want to become a great dancer, don't you?"

"Yes," I said through my tears.

"All right, then. Greatness means that people may laugh at you. You might make a mistake, and everyone will laugh. Sometimes people will clap wildly after you dance. At other times they won't clap at all. Sometimes you work for a lot of money. Then, again, you may work for almost nothing at all.

"If you're a true dancer, you will keep on working very hard. For an hour or two, you will make the people who watch you forget their sadness and their problems. This is a great thing."

Today I am grown up. But I still remember Anna Pavlova and the words she spoke to me. She taught me that a ballet dancer must do more than dance well. A dancer must also care about the people watching. And he or she must never give up.

MARGO AND PAVLOVA   *cause/effect*

Circle the letter of the best answer to each question.

1. Why did Margo cry after she had danced?
   a. She was very tired.
   (b.) Her long underwear fell down.

2. Why was Pavlova sad?
   (a.) Her dog had died.
   b. The people did not clap for her.

3. What made Pavlova feel happy again?
   (a.) She was paid a lot of money for being in the ballet.
   b. Margo's costume made her laugh.

⟜ *42 • Best Score 3 • My Score* _____

MARGO'S FEELINGS   *classification/outline*

Write A before the sentences that show Margo was happy. Write B before the sentences that show she was unhappy.

__A__ How lucky I was!
__A__ It was time to meet Anna Pavlova.

48

_A_ "Yes," I said through my tears.
_B_ I had been dancing the whole time in this silly costume.

⟜ 86 • *Best Score 4 • My Score* _____

A GREAT DANCER *generalizations*

Circle the numerals of the three things that Margo learned are most important to a great ballet dancer.

1. being rich
2. doing ballet steps correctly
3. resting instead of working too hard
4. making people forget their troubles
5. not giving up

⟜ 77 • *Best Score 3 • My Score* _____

All Best Scores 10 • All My Scores _____

MARGO'S STORY *comparison/contrast*

Tell about a time something has happened to you that made you feel silly or sad. What good came of your experience? What did you learn from it?

I learned that at ballet was not so easy and have lots of troble like Margo.

49

Key Words
scarecrows
straw
post

Summer Scarecrows

by Avon Neal

The scarecrows on these pages look almost alive. Some animals believe they are!

A scarecrow does just what its name says. It scares crows from a farmer's field. Scarecrows also frighten away other animals. If it weren't for these straw-filled friends, animals would eat the seeds and vegetables that the farmer has planted.

How do you make a scarecrow? First put a post in the ground. That will be the scarecrow's body. Then nail a piece of wood across the post, near the top. That will be the scarecrow's arms.

Now comes the fun part. What kind of clothes will your scarecrow wear? Overalls and a shirt, a dress, a hat, gloves, a scarf that will flutter in the wind? Once you have dressed your scarecrow, stuff the clothes with straw. Tie the clothes at the bottom so the straw doesn't fall out.

The only thing your scarecrow is missing now is a head. For this, you might use an old broom, a mop or any round object. Paint on a face

52

if you like, and presto! You have yourself a scarecrow.

Some farmers say that scarecrows do a great job of scaring away unwanted animals. Others say a smart animal like a crow will soon figure out that scarecrows are only made of straw. Whether or not scarecrows really scare off animals, one thing is certain. Scarecrows are fun to make and fun to look at.

53

DO IT RIGHT *sequence*

The sentences below tell how to make a
scarecrow. Write 1 before the first step,
2 before the second step and so on.

_4_ Add an old broom, a mop or any
round object, and paint on a face.
_3_ Dress the scarecrow and stuff it
with straw.
_1_ Put a post in the ground.
_2_ Nail a piece of wood across the
post, near the top.

⚷ 105 · *Best Score 4 · My Score* _____

SCARECROWS *author's purpose*

Check (✔) the three sentences that
sum up the most important things the
writer wanted to tell you about
scarecrows.

_✔_ a. A scarf will flutter in the wind.
_✔_ b. Scarecrows help farmers.
_____ c. Scarecrows should wear
overalls.
_✔_ d. Scarecrows seem almost alive.

54

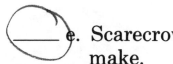_____ e. Scarecrows are fairly easy to make.

🔑 73 • *Best Score 3* • *My Score* _____

STRAW TALK *fact/opinion*

Put 1 before each fact. Put 2 before each opinion.

__1__ Dressing a scarecrow is fun.

__2__ The purpose of a scarecrow is to frighten away animals from a farmer's fields.

__1__ Scarecrows do a great job of scaring away unwanted animals.

🔑 45 • *Best Score 3* • *My Score* _____

All Best Scores 10 • *All My Scores* _____

HOW WOULD IT LOOK? *aesthetics*

If you were to make a scarecrow, what would you make it look like? Would it seem happy, sad, scary, nice? How would you dress it? Give reasons for your answers. I would seem sad to just stay their all the time.

Key Words

dinosaur
Uncompahgre
Plateau
Colorado
dig
supersaurus

Dinosaur Jim and

by Jean George

It was a moonlit night in August
1972. "Dinosaur Jim" Jensen crawled
out of his tent. He wanted to take just
one more look at what he had found.

Jim Jensen studies dinosaurs
(DY-nuh-sors). He, his son and a helper
were camped on the Uncompahgre
Plateau (un-kum-PAH-gray pla-TOH)
in Colorado.

56

UNITED STATES

Colorado

Uncompahgre ★
Plateau

the Supersaurus

One hundred and fifty million years ago, the Uncompahgre Plateau was not dry, as it is today. There used to be lots of rain, swamps and forests. It was very warm. Dinosaurs as tall as trees or smaller than chickens roamed the plateau. Some ate meat. Others ate plants. Some dinosaurs flew in the sky. Some lived in the water. Others walked on land.

Dinosaur Jim and his team had been searching for dinosaur bones. The place in which people like Dinosaur Jim look for such bones is called a *dig*. Jim and his special team of searchers had discovered the bones of many kinds of animals which no one had ever known about. But the biggest find of the Uncompahgre dig was the bones of a dinosaur called supersaurus (soo-per-SOR-us).

Supersaurus was the largest dinosaur of all. It was the biggest land animal that ever lived, too.

It was 80 feet (24.38 meters) long. It weighed at least 75 tons (about 68 metric tons). That's about as heavy as 26 cars. It was extra tall. It could have looked in the top-floor windows of a five-story building.

Supersaurus was as dumb as it was big. It had a very tiny and simple brain. So it acted mostly without thinking.

Supersaurus may have been a giant. But it was quite gentle. It ate plants. It liked leaves from treetops.

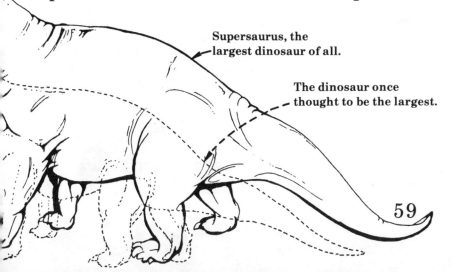

Supersaurus, the largest dinosaur of all.

The dinosaur once thought to be the largest.

59

Dinosaur Jim enjoys studying dinosaurs. To him, finding and putting together the bones of a new animal such as supersaurus is one of the most exciting things in the world. Piece by piece, the bones are linked together with steel rods. After months, or even years, the creature stands in a museum.

"My dream is to build a new kind of museum," Dinosaur Jim says. "I would build it right up the side of a dig. People would get into an elevator at the bottom of the dig. They would ride up past each layer of rock. The bones of animals from the past are in those layers. I would have all these animals shown right where they lived and died."

Dinosaur Jim's dream may come true. If it does, you may someday visit one of his museum digs. If supersaurus is there, you won't miss it. Just look for the biggest dinosaur of them all.

Dinosaur Jim with the world's longest dinosaur rib.

61

THAT'S SUPERSAURUS *figurative language*

Circle the word that best fits each blank.

Supersaurus was as _____ as 26 cars.
   (a.) heavy b. colorful c. noisy

It was so _____, it could have looked in the fifth-floor window of a building.
   (a.) tall b. fat c. curious

Supersaurus was as _____ as it was big.
   a. fast b. smart (c.) dumb

🔑 *50 • Best Score 3 • My Score* _____

MANY YEARS AGO *paragraph meaning*

Read the third paragraph in the story. Then circle two answers that complete each sentence.

1. Uncompahgre Plateau was _____.
    a. dry   c. warm
    (b.) rainy   d. cold

2. Dinosaurs _____.
    a. were of many different sizes.
    (b.) lived in the water, on land and in the air.

62

c. liked dry plateaus.
d. were tamed by people.

☞ 14 • *Best Score 4 • My Score* _____

BIG IDEAS   *main idea*

Check (✔) the three most important ideas in the story.

___✓___ 1. Dinosaur Jim has found important dinosaur bones.

_____ 2. Dinosaur Jim crawled out of his tent one moonlit night.

_____ 3. Some dinosaurs ate meat.

___✓___ 4. Supersaurus was a fantastic animal.

___✓___ 5. Dinosaur museums may someday be built at the digs.

☞ 76 • *Best Score 3 • My Score* _____

All Best Scores 10 • All My Scores _____

IMPORTANT TO YOU   *comparison/contrast*

Finding supersaurus was very important to Dinosaur Jim. Tell about a time when you found something that was important to you. I think dinosaur's bones are important and learning lia Jim.

Key Words

pigeons
loft

Racers with Wings

by Corrado Pallenberg

It was early morning. The race was about to begin. The racers sat calmly in their baskets. Their owners walked back and forth, waiting for starting time.

And then it came. The baskets were opened. The noise was like 1000 people opening newspapers at the same time. More than 5000 wings flashed in the morning sun. Pigeons rose into the air together like a great cloud. Then they circled and headed north. The pigeon race was on! After 11 hours and 49 minutes, the winning pigeon found its way home to its *loft*.

Races like this happen all over the world. About a million people take part in the sport. Some own only 20 pigeons, and some own more than 100.

To most people, a racing pigeon looks like any pigeon you might see in a park. But people who race pigeons can tell the difference. A racer has a stronger neck and wings. It can see very well from high up.

Usually whole families help take care of the racing pigeons. Every day the pigeon loft has to be cleaned. The pigeons need food twice a day. They need clean water even more often. The pigeons live, lay their eggs and raise their young in the loft.

A pigeon owner starts training a bird when the bird is about 45 days old. At first the bird is taken only a short

way from its loft. Then it is called back and given some food. Little by little, the pigeon is taken farther away. Each time it must find its way back home. Soon it is ready to race.

In a race, all the pigeons are let go from one place. Then each bird must find its way back to its own loft. Special maps show the birds' starting place and the location of their lofts. Special clocks are used to time the birds.

How do birds find their way home from so far away? No one knows for sure. But many people think the pigeons may use the sun as a guide. When the sky is cloudy, pigeons don't race well. They may fly into telephone wires. In storms or fog, they sometimes get lost.

Pigeons love their homes and families. A pigeon flies especially fast if it has young pigeons back in the loft. It wants to get home to care for them.

Grown-up pigeons make friends with each other. Once two pigeons named Dollar Princess and Grand Prize flew a long race in bad weather. Dollar Princess got back to the loft, but Grand Prize didn't.

68

The next morning, their owner was cleaning the loft. The weather was still bad. Dollar Princess got out and flew off through the rain and wind. Many hours passed. The owner wondered if she was lost, too.

Late that afternoon, Dollar Princess came flying back with Grand Prize beside her. Somehow she had found her friend and brought him safely home.

THE RACE BEGINS   *paragraph meaning*

Circle the word that belongs in each blank.

1. The race began in the _____.
   a. evening (b.) morning

2. The pigeons were kept in _____ just before the race started.
   a. (baskets) b. lofts

3. The start of a pigeon race sounds like 1000 people opening _____.
   a. doors (b.) newspapers

4. The pigeons flew _____.
   (a.) north   b. south

5. The race took over _____ hours.
   (a.) 11   b. 49

6. A loft is a pigeon's _____.
   (a.) home   b. wing size

175 • *Best Score 6* • *My Score* _____

ZOOMING IN   *supporting details*

Read the first sentence in each group. Circle the letters of two sentences that

70

show the first sentence is true.

1. Pigeons can feel <u>love</u>.
   - a. A racing pigeon often has trouble flying when there are clouds or fog.
   - b. Dollar Princess helped her friend Grand Prize find his way home.
   - c. A racing pigeon flies faster if it has young at home.

2. It is hard work to <u>take care</u> of racing pigeons.
   - a. Every day the pigeon loft has to be cleaned.
   - b. The pigeons need food twice a day.
   - c. A racing pigeon can see very well from high up.

☞ *90 • Best Score 4 • My Score* _____

All Best Scores 10 • All My Scores _____

RACING AS A SPORT *comparison/contrast*

Pigeon racing is just one kind of racing sport. Name other kinds of races. Which is your favorite? Why? Hores races because there are hores in it and they are big and strong.

The Friendly Skies of 2026

by Andrew M. de Voursney

Billy Parker lives in the year 2026. Planes are still carrying people from city to city. But there are many changes. Let's follow Billy and his mother. They are going to visit Billy's grandfather in California.

Key Words

computer
flights
reserve
tickets
airport, airline

Mrs. Parker walked over to her computer. It sat in one corner of the living room. She pressed a few buttons. Out came a list of plane flights from Chicago to San Francisco.

"Why don't we go on the 12:30 flight?" she said to Billy. She pushed some more buttons to reserve two seats on that plane. In just a few seconds, two tickets zipped out of the computer.

Later that morning it began to rain. "Will our plane be able to take off if it's raining?" asked Billy.

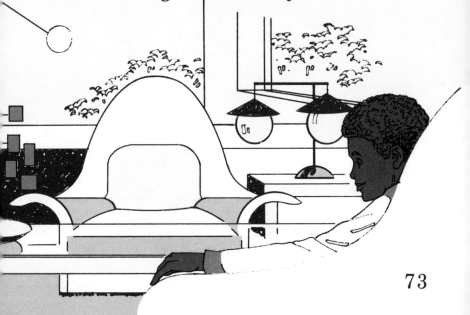

"Of course," said Mrs. Parker. "Airports have special controls that keep away bad weather so planes can land and take off."

Mrs. Parker and Billy got into a taxicab. The driver pushed three buttons, and the cab zoomed toward the airport. The cab never touched the ground.

Mrs. Parker and Billy went into the main building. Mrs. Parker put their tickets and a special card into a check-in computer. The computer clicked away. Then it spoke.

"Good day, Mrs. Parker and Billy.

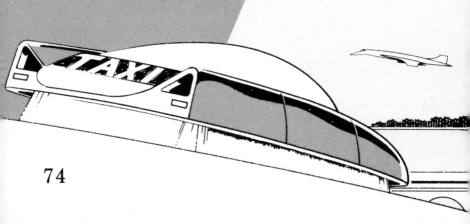

You will be leaving on our 12:30 flight to San Francisco, California. You will have seats 20 H and 21 H. The cost of the flight from Chicago to San Francisco for two people is $1,640. I have just taken the money from your bank.

"There are lots of nice shops on the second floor. If you wish to look at the planes landing and taking off, you may go up on the roof. If you have any questions or problems, one of the computers or airline people will be glad to help. Have a good flight."

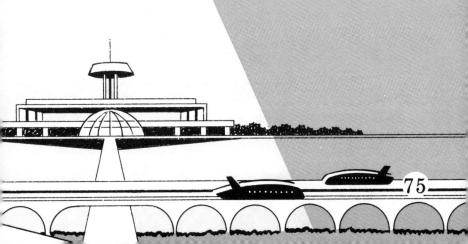

"Mom, let's go up to the roof and watch the planes," said Billy.

When they reached the roof, they saw how busy the airport was. Mrs. Parker tried to answer Billy's questions about the different kinds of planes.

"That small plane is called a Bomac 600. It holds 250 people. It is used for short distances.

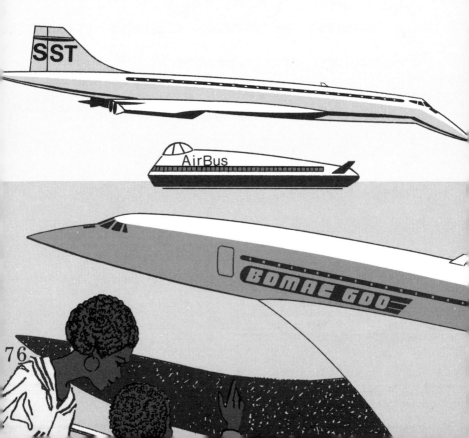

"That one landing is an SST. It carries 500 people. The SST flies between cities that are very far away. So it has to fly very fast. It can fly faster than the speed of sound! A long time ago, back in the 1970s, a plane traveling that fast made a big, booming noise. The noise could be heard by people on the ground. But today an SST makes hardly any noise at all."

"What is that thing over there?" asked Billy. "It looks like a bus."

"It is. It's an airbus. It rides on a layer of air. It's used between cities and towns that are near each other."

"What kind of plane will we fly in to visit Grandpa?" Billy asked.

"Do you see that huge plane over there? That's a Bomac 900, and that's what we will be flying in. It's extra wide and holds 1,700 people.

"A long time ago, people used to ride just in the center of a plane. But the double-decker Bomac 900 has seats in the wings. Each wing has 12 sections. There are 72 seats in each section. People walk from the airport's main building directly into the wings. The people don't have to stay in their seats. They can relax in the sitting rooms in

78

the wings. The wings also hold the kitchens in which the airline people make the food."

Just then a voice announced, "All those with tickets on the 12:30 flight to San Francisco, please go to Gate 101. Have a pleasant flight."

"Let's go, Billy," said Mrs. Parker. "We'll be seeing Grandpa in California before you know it."

Billy gave one last look at all the wonderful planes. Then he smiled and wondered, "What will planes be like 50 years from now, in the year 2076?"

NAME THE PLANE   *classification/outline*

Write the numeral of the name of each plane in the blank next to its description.

1. airbus
2. Bomac 600
3. SST
4. Bomac 900

__2__ People sit in its wings.
__3__ It flies fast and far.
__1__ It rides on a layer of air.
__4__ It flies short distances.

☞ 105 • *Best Score 4* • *My Score* _____

PLANE TALK   *vocabulary*

Write the numeral of the word that belongs in each sentence.

1. computer   3. ticket
2. reserve   4. flight

A __1__ is a machine that gives you information and can almost think.

When you __2__ a seat, you are asking an airline to save room for you.

80

To get on a plane, you need a special piece of paper called a __3__.

A __3__ is a plane trip between two cities.

☞ 104 • Best Score 4 • My Score _____

TODAY AND TOMORROW *fact/opinion*

Check (✔) two items below that name things we see around us <u>today</u>.

___✔___ 1. home computers
___✔___ 2. airports
_____ 3. complete weather control
_____ 4. speaking airport computers
_____ 5. taxicabs that ride on air
_____ 6. planes that fly from city to city

☞ 39 • Best Score 2 • My Score _____
All Best Scores 10 • All My Scores _____

2076 *predicting*

At the end of the story, Billy wondered what planes would be like in the year 2076. What do you think they will be like then? I think it will be like round and big and hevey slowe and some are sarp lite and fast.

81

Key Words

champion
skaters, skates
skating
rink
contest

Champion on Ice

*by Phyllis and
Zander Hollander*

The eight-year-old girl watched the skaters spin and twirl in the ice show. She turned to her father and mother and said, "I want to be a skater."

That Christmas, Tenley Albright found new ice skates beneath the Christmas tree. Soon after, she began taking skating lessons. She practiced every day.

Most of Tenley's friends could not skate. So she spent a lot of time alone.

But Tenley did not mind being alone. She told herself, "Someday I will be a skating champion."

One day something happened to Tenley that made her stop skating. She became very sick. Her legs became stiff. She could not walk.

She was taken to a hospital. The doctors there taught her how to move

her legs again. Tenley had to work hard
to walk again. At last she was back on
her skates.

Every day, she practiced at the
skating rink. She dreamed of winning a
skating contest.

It wasn't long before her dream
came true. Tenley won first prize in a
contest for young skaters. From then
on, she won contests all over the world.

But Tenley did not forget about
the doctors in the hospital. She knew

how much they had helped her. She
wanted to help other people get well.
She decided to become a doctor.

Now Tenley is a doctor. She works
hard in a hospital. She helps many
people. Some days she leaves work
feeling very tired.

But Tenley doesn't always go right
home. She takes her ice skates and
heads for the nearest skating rink!
There she spins and glides the way she
did when she was a skating champion.

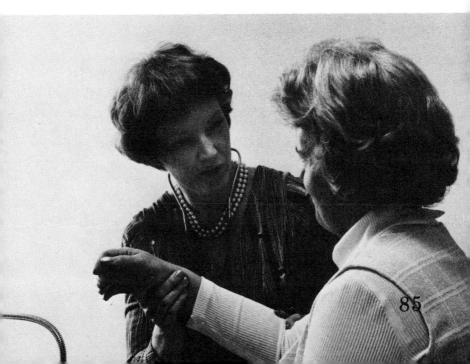

NEW WORDS *vocabulary*

Circle the best word.

1. A person who wins prizes is a _____.
   a. skater (b.) champion

2. Skaters try to win prizes in a _____.
   a. lesson b. (contest)

3. An ice floor is called a _____.
   a. pond (b.) rink

4. Doctors work in a _____.
   a. contest (b.) hospital

⌐○ *85 • Best Score 4 • My Score* _____

TELL WHY *cause/effect*

Circle the letter of each right answer.

1. What made Tenley want to skate?
   (a.) She saw an ice show.
   b. Her parents made her take
      skating lessons.

2. Why did Tenley stop skating?
   a. She had to go to school.
   (b.) She became very sick.

3. Why did Tenley become the best

86

skater in the world?

    a. She had special skates.

    (b.) She practiced every day.

🗝 41 · *Best Score 3* · *My Score* _____

DR. ALBRIGHT   *characterization*

Check (✔) three sentences that tell about Tenley Albright.

_____ 1. Her parents didn't want her to skate.

_____ 2. She tries hard at everything she does.

_____ 3. She stopped skating after she became a doctor.

_____ 4. She won prizes in skating contests.

_____ 5. She works in a hospital.

_____ 6. She still cannot walk.

🗝 77 · *Best Score 3* · *My Score* _____

All Best Scores 10 · *All My Scores* _____

PRACTICE! PRACTICE!   *analogy*

Do you practice anything? What? How does practice help you? I have to pratic piano and if you pratice you get beter at thing that you praticed.

87

Flash Flood!

by Pat Mills,
as told to Rosemary Munday

Key Words
flash flood
creek
riverbank
drowned

A fork of lightning jabbed the dark sky. Thunder shook the ground. Rain began to pour down.

Mrs. Mills was driving home from the swimming pool with her two sons, five-year-old Terry and three-year-old David. As she neared home, she had to

slow down the car and stop. Ahead of her was Benson's Creek. All this rain had turned the small creek into a fast-moving river. The water completely covered the road.

Mrs. Mills let the car crawl forward. She was thinking, "If the water isn't too deep, I can inch the car across the road."

But as her car got about halfway across, Mrs. Mills saw that the water was much deeper than she had thought. The water rose higher. It lifted the car up a little and moved it sideways. Mrs. Mills knew she and the children had to get out of the car.

But the water was pushing the doors shut. So Mrs. Mills grabbed little David. The two of them climbed out the window.

The water was up to Mrs. Mills' knees. She wanted to leave David on dry ground while she went back to the car to get Terry.

But she and David didn't reach dry ground in time. A flash flood came roaring down on them. The angry brown water pushed them under for a moment. Then they bobbed to the top. Mrs. Mills grabbed some of the bushes near the riverbank and pulled herself and David to safety.

Then she turned and looked back at the car. The river was taking it downstream! In the half-light, she could see Terry's frightened face looking out the back window. The car was washed around a bend in the river and was lost from sight.

Mrs. Mills still held David in her arms. She ran up the road to get help. Soon police, friends and neighbors started a search for Terry. All night they looked along the creek. At last they found the car, but Terry was nowhere to be seen. Had he drowned in the flood, or had he made it to dry ground? No one knew.

The next morning, Mr. and Mrs. Mills sat in their home. They heard the blast of car horns outside. Then there was shouting. Mr. and Mrs. Mills rushed outside.

"Terry is alive," said one woman. "He's all right! He's in town at Mrs. Santos' home."

Mr. and Mrs. Mills drove into town to get their son. When they arrived at the Santos house, Terry was in the kitchen quietly eating bacon and eggs.

"Hello," he said. "Why is everyone crying?"

"We thought you had drowned in Benson's Creek," explained Mrs. Mills. "They were looking for you all night. What happened?"

"The car got stuck on two trees that had fallen over," Terry said. "So I went out one of the back windows. I

crawled away from the river on one of the tree trunks."

"Then I got lost. But I kept going. At last I saw lots of lights. I thought some farmers were working in their fields."

"Terry, those weren't farmers working," explained Mr. Mills. "They were people searching for <u>you</u>."

"I didn't know that, Dad," Terry said. "I didn't want to bother them. So I went to sleep in the bushes until morning. When I got up, I saw a lot of people looking for something. I wanted to help them, so I started looking, too."

"Why didn't someone see Terry?" Mr. Mills asked.

"Probably because no one expects a lost person to be part of a search group," answered Mrs. Mills. She turned to Terry. "How did they find you?"

"Mr. Walker found me," Terry said. "You know him. He has a farm near our house. He was one of the people looking for me.

"I saw some sandwiches on the front seat of his truck. I was so hungry! Mr. Walker came up to me. He asked me what my name was. I told him. He was so surprised, he almost fell into the truck!"

"Well, Terry, are you ready to go home now?" Mrs. Mills asked.

"Just a minute, Mom. I want to finish my bacon and eggs."

WORDS THAT POINT   *signals/antecedents*

Pick the person or persons each underlined word stands for. Write the numeral in the blank.

1. the searchers   3. Mrs. Mills
2. Mrs. Mills and David 4. Terry

___4___ "Mr. Walker came up to <u>me</u>."

___3___ Then <u>she</u> turned and looked back at the car.

___1___ All night <u>they</u> looked along the creek.

___2___ A flash flood came roaring down on <u>them</u>.

🔑105 • *Best Score 4* • *My Score* _____

WORD PICTURES   *figurative language*

Match each word picture with the missing word in the sentences on the next page. Write the letters in the blanks.

a.

b.

c.

A __a__ of lightning jabbed the sky.

"If the water isn't too deep, I can __b__ the car across."

A flash flood came __c__ down on them.

🗝 52 • *Best Score 3* • *My Score* _____

FRONT PAGE NEWS   *summary*

Check (✔) three newspaper headlines that best sum up the story.

____✔ 1. Boy Found After Flash Flood
____✔ 2. Heavy Rains Wash Away Car and Young Boy
____ 3. Mr. Walker Joins Searchers
____✔ 4. Woman and Children Almost Killed in Flood

🗝 66 • *Best Score 3* • *My Score* _____

All Best Scores 10 • *All My Scores* _____

TERRY   *inferences*

How did Terry feel when the flood took the car downstream? How did he feel when his parents came to take him home? How did you know?

96

I feeled if Terry was going to get killed and when he was found I think Terry felt glad to go home.